TRANZLATY

Language is for everyone

اللغة للجميع

Aladdin and the Wonderful Lamp

علاء الدين والمصباح الرائع

Antoine Galland

أنطوان جالاند

English / العربية

Copyright © 2025 Tranzlaty
All rights reserved
Published by Tranzlaty
ISBN: 978-1-83566-913-6
Original text by Antoine Galland
From *"Les mille et une nuits"*
First published in French in 1704
Taken from The Blue Fairy Book
Collected and translated by Andrew Lang
www.tranzlaty.com

Once upon a time there lived a poor tailor
ذات مرة كان هناك خياط فقير

this poor tailor had a son called Aladdin
كان لهذا الخياط الفقير ابن اسمه علاء الدين

Aladdin was a careless, idle boy who did nothing
كان علاء الدين فتىً مهملًا خاملًا لا يفعل شيئًا

although, he did like to play ball all day long
على الرغم من ذلك، كان يحب لعب الكرة طوال اليوم

this he did in the streets with other little idle boys
لقد فعل هذا في الشوارع مع الأولاد الصغار العاطلين عن العمل

This so grieved the father that he died
لقد حزن الأب كثيرًا حتى مات

his mother cried and prayed, but nothing helped
بكت أمه وصليت ولكن لم ينفعها شيء

despite her pleading, Aladdin did not mend his ways
على الرغم من توسلاتها، لم يقم علاء الدين بإصلاح طرقه

One day, Aladdin was playing in the streets, as usual
ذات يوم كان علاء الدين يلعب في الشوارع كعادته

a stranger asked him his age
ساله غريب عن عمره

and he asked him, "are you not the son of Mustapha the tailor?"
فسأله :ألست ابن مصطفى الخياط؟

"I am the son of Mustapha, sir," replied Aladdin
"أنا ابن مصطفى يا سيدي "رد علاء الدين

"but he died a long time ago"
"لكنه مات منذ زمن طويل "

the stranger was a famous African magician
كان الغريب ساحرًا أفريقيًا مشهورًا

and he fell on his neck and kissed him
ووقع على عنقه وقبله

"I am your uncle," said the magician
"أنا عمك "قال الساحر

"I knew you from your likeness to my brother"
"عرفتك من شبهك بأخي "

"Go to your mother and tell her I am coming"

- 1 -

"اذهب إلى والدتك وأخبرها أنني قادم"

Aladdin ran home and told his mother of his newly found uncle

ركض علاء الدين إلى منزله وأخبر والدته عن عمه الذي وجده حديثًا

"Indeed, child," she said, "your father had a brother"

قالت: يا بني، إن لأبيك أخًا .

"but I always thought he was dead"

"لكنني اعتقدت دائمًا أنه ميت"

However, she prepared supper for the visitor

ولكنها أعدت العشاء للزائر

and she bade Aladdin to seek his uncle

وطلبت من علاء الدين أن يبحث عن عمه

Aladdin's uncle came laden with wine and fruit

جاء عم علاء الدين محملاً بالنبيذ والفواكه

He fell down and kissed the place where Mustapha used to sit

سقط على الأرض وقبل المكان الذي كان يجلس فيه مصطفى

and he bid Aladdin's mother not to be surprised

وطلب من أم علاء الدين ألا تتفاجأ

he explained he had been out of the country for forty years

وأوضح أنه كان خارج البلاد لمدة أربعين عامًا

He then turned to Aladdin and asked him his trade

ثم التفت إلى علاء الدين وسأله عن تجارته

but the boy hung his head in shame

لكن الصبي أطرق رأسه خجلاً

and his mother burst into tears

وانفجرت والدته بالبكاء

so Aladdin's uncle offered to provide food

لذلك عرض عم علاء الدين توفير الطعام

The next day he bought Aladdin a fine set of clothes

وفي اليوم التالي اشترى علاء الدين مجموعة رائعة من الملابس

and he took him all over the city

وأخذه في جميع أنحاء المدينة

he showed him the sights of the city

أظهر له معالم المدينة

at nightfall he brought him home to his mother

وعند حلول الليل أحضره إلى منزل والدته

his mother was overjoyed to see her son so well dressed

كانت والدته سعيدة للغاية عندما رأت ابنها يرتدي ملابس أنيقة

The next day the magician led Aladdin into some beautiful gardens

في اليوم التالي، قاد الساحر علاء الدين إلى بعض الحدائق الجميلة

this was a long way outside the city gates

كانت هذه مسافة طويلة خارج أبواب المدينة

They sat down by a fountain

جلسوا بجانب النافورة

and the magician pulled a cake from his girdle

وأخرج الساحر كعكة من حزامه

he divided the cake between the two of them

قام بتقسيم الكعكة بينهما

Then they journeyed onward till they almost reached the mountains

ثم واصلوا رحلتهم حتى كادوا يصلون إلى الجبال

Aladdin was so tired that he begged to go back

كان علاء الدين متعبًا جدًا لدرجة أنه توسل للعودة

but the magician beguiled him with pleasant stories

ولكن الساحر أغواه بقصص لطيفة

and he led him on in spite of his laziness

وقاده على الرغم من كسله

At last they came to two mountains

وأخيرا وصلوا إلى جبلين

the two mountains were divided by a narrow valley

تم فصل الجبلين بواسطة واد ضيق

"We will go no farther," said the false uncle

"لن نذهب أبعد من ذلك" قال العم الكاذب

"I will show you something wonderful"

"سأريك شيئا رائعا"

"gather up sticks, while I kindle a fire"

"اجمعوا الحطب بينما أشعل النار"

When the fire was lit the magician threw a powder on it

عندما أشعلت النار ألقى الساحر عليها مسحوقًا

and he said some magical words

وقال بعض الكلمات السحرية

The earth trembled a little and opened in front of them

ارتجفت الأرض قليلا وانفتحت أمامهم

a square flat stone revealed itself

كشف حجر مسطح مربع عن نفسه

and in the middle of the stone was a brass ring

وفي وسط الحجر كان هناك حلقة من النحاس

Aladdin tried to run away

حاول علاء الدين الهرب

but the magician caught him

لكن الساحر أمسكه

and gave him a blow that knocked him down

وأعطاه ضربة أسقطته أرضًا

"What have I done, uncle?" he said, piteously

"ماذا فعلت يا عم؟ "قال بحزن

the magician said more kindly, "Fear nothing, but obey me"

قال الساحر بلباقة أكبر" :لا تخف من شيء، ولكن أطعني ."

"Beneath this stone lies a treasure which is to be yours"

"تحت هذا الحجر يوجد كنز سيكون ملكك "

"and no one else may touch this treasure"

"ولا يجوز لأحد آخر أن يلمس هذا الكنز "

"so you must do exactly as I tell you"

"لذا يجب عليك أن تفعل بالضبط كما أقول لك "

At the mention of treasure Aladdin forgot his fears

عند ذكر الكنز نسي علاء الدين مخاوفه

he grasped the ring as he was told

أمسك بالخاتم كما قيل له

and he said the names of his father and grandfather

وقال اسمي أبيه وجده

The stone came up quite easily

لقد جاء الحجر بسهولة تامة

and some steps appeared in front of them

وظهرت أمامهم بعض الخطوات

"Go down," said the magician

"انزل "قال الساحر

"at the foot of those steps you will find an open door"

"عند أسفل تلك الخطوات ستجد بابًا مفتوحًا "
"the door leads into three large halls"
"الباب يؤدي إلى ثلاث قاعات كبيرة "
"Tuck up your gown and go through the halls"
"ارفعي ثوبك واذهبي إلى القاعات "
"make sure not to touch anything"
"تأكد من عدم لمس أي شيء "
"if you touch anything, you will instantly die"
"إذا لمست أي شيء، سوف تموت على الفور "
"These halls lead into a garden of fine fruit trees"
"هذه القاعات تؤدي إلى حديقة مليئة بأشجار الفاكهة الجميلة "
"Walk on until you reach a gap in the terrace"
"استمر في المشي حتى تصل إلى فجوة في الشرفة "
"there you will see a lighted lamp"
"ستجد هناك مصباحًا مضاءً "
"Pour out the oil of the lamp"
"صبوا زيت المصباح "
"and then bring me the lamp"
"ثم أحضر لي المصباح "
He drew a ring from his finger and gave it to Aladdin
أخرج خاتمًا من إصبعه وأعطاه لعلاء الدين
and he bid him to prosper
وأمره بالنجاح
Aladdin found everything as the magician had said
وجد علاء الدين كل شيء كما قال الساحر
he gathered some fruit off the trees
لقد جمع بعض الفاكهة من الأشجار
and, having got the lamp, he arrived at the mouth of the cave
وبعد أن حصل على المصباح وصل إلى فم الكهف
The magician cried out in a great hurry
صرخ الساحر بسرعة كبيرة
"Make haste and give me the lamp"
"أسرع وأعطني المصباح "
Aladdin refused to do this until he was out of the cave
رفض علاء الدين القيام بذلك حتى خرج من الكهف
The magician flew into a terrible rage

لقد طار الساحر في غضب رهيب

he threw some more powder on to the fire

ألقى المزيد من البارود على النار

and then he cast another magic spell

ثم ألقى تعويذة سحرية أخرى

and the stone rolled back into its place

ودحرج الحجر إلى مكانه

The magician left Persia for ever

لقد غادر الساحر بلاد فارس إلى الأبد

this plainly showed that he was no uncle of Aladdin's

وهذا يدل بوضوح على أنه لم يكن عم علاء الدين .

what he really was was a cunning magician

ما كان عليه في الحقيقة هو ساحر ماكر

a magician who had read of a magic lamp

ساحر قرأ عن المصباح السحري

a magic lamp which would make him the most powerful man in the world

مصباح سحري سيجعله الرجل الأقوى في العالم

but he alone knew where to find the magic lamp

ولكنه وحده كان يعرف أين يجد المصباح السحري

and he could only receive the magic lamp from the hand of another

ولم يكن بوسعه أن يحصل على المصباح السحري إلا من يد شخص آخر .

He had picked out the foolish Aladdin for this purpose

لقد اختار علاء الدين الأحمق لهذا الغرض

he had intended to get the magical lamp and kill him afterwards

كان ينوي الحصول على المصباح السحري وقتله بعد ذلك

For two days Aladdin remained in the dark

بقي علاء الدين في الظلام لمدة يومين

he cried and lamented his situation

بكى وندب حاله

At last he clasped his hands in prayer

وأخيرا صفق بيديه في الصلاة

and in so doing he rubbed the ring

وبذلك قام بفرك الخاتم

the magician had forgotten to take the ring back from him

لقد نسي الساحر أن يأخذ الخاتم منه

Immediately an enormous and frightful genie rose out of the earth

وفجأة خرج من الأرض جن ضخم ومرعب

"What would thou have me do?"

"ماذا تريد مني أن أفعل؟"

"I am the Slave of the Ring"

"أنا عبد الخاتم"

"and I will obey thee in all things"

"وسأطيعك في كل شيء"

Aladdin fearlessly replied: "Deliver me from this place!"

فأجاب علاء الدين بلا خوف: "نجني من هذا المكان"!

and the earth opened above him

وانفتحت الأرض فوقه

and he found himself outside

ووجد نفسه بالخارج

As soon as his eyes could bear the light he went home

بمجرد أن أصبحت عيناه قادرة على تحمل الضوء، ذهب إلى منزله

but he fainted when he got there

ولكنه أغمي عليه عندما وصل هناك

When he came to himself he told his mother what had happened

عندما عاد إلى نفسه أخبر أمه بما حدث

and he showed her the lamp

وأظهر لها المصباح

and he showed her the fruits he had gathered in the garden

وأظهر لها الثمار التي جمعها في الحديقة

the fruits were, in reality, precious stones

وكانت الثمار في الحقيقة أحجاراً ثمينة

He then asked for some food

ثم طلب بعض الطعام

"Alas! child," she said

"آه يا بني" قالت

"I have no food in the house"

"ليس لدي طعام في المنزل"

"but I have spun a little cotton"

"but I have spun a little cotton"
"لكنني غزلت القليل من القطن"
"and I will go and sell the cotton"
"وسأذهب وأبيع القطن"
Aladdin bade her keep her cotton
أمرها علاء الدين بالاحتفاظ بقطنها
he told her he would sell the magic lamp instead of the cotton
أخبرها أنه سيبيع المصباح السحري بدلاً من القطن
As it was very dirty she began to rub the magic lamp
وبما أنها كانت متسخة جدًا، بدأت في فرك المصباح السحري
a clean magic lamp might fetch a higher price
قد يكون سعر المصباح السحري النظيف أعلى
Instantly a hideous genie appeared
فجأة ظهر جني بشع
he asked what she would like to have
سألها ماذا تريد أن تحصل عليه
at the sight of the genie she fainted
عند رؤية الجني أغمي عليها
but Aladdin, snatching the magic lamp, said boldly:
لكن علاء الدين انتزع المصباح السحري وقال بجرأة :
"Fetch me something to eat!"
"أحضر لي شيئًا لأكله"!
The genie returned with a silver bowl
عاد الجني مع وعاء فضي
he had twelve silver plates containing rich meats
كان لديه اثنا عشر طبقًا فضيًا تحتوي على لحوم غنية
and he had two silver cups and two bottles of wine
وكان معه كأسان من الفضة وزجاجتان من النبيذ
Aladdin's mother, when she came to herself, said:
أم علاء الدين عندما أفاقت من غفلتها قالت :
"Whence comes this splendid feast?"
"من أين يأتي هذا العيد الرائع؟ "
"Ask not where this food came from, but eat, mother," replied Aladdin
"لا تسألي من أين جاء هذا الطعام، بل كليه يا أمي" أجاب علاء الدين
So they sat at breakfast till it was dinner-time

فجلسوا يتناولون الفطور حتى حان وقت العشاء

and Aladdin told his mother about the magic lamp

وأخبر علاء الدين أمه عن المصباح السحري

She begged him to sell the magic lamp

توسلت إليه أن يبيع المصباح السحري

"let us have nothing to do with devils"

"لا ينبغي لنا أن نتعامل مع الشياطين"

but Aladdin had thought it would be wiser to use the magic lamp

لكن علاء الدين كان يعتقد أنه سيكون من الحكمة استخدام المصباح السحري

"chance hath made us aware of the magic lamp's virtues"

"لقد جعلتنا الصدفة ندرك فضائل المصباح السحري"

"we will use the magic lamp, and we will use the ring"

"سوف نستخدم المصباح السحري، وسوف نستخدم الخاتم"

"I shall always wear the ring on my finger"

"سوف أرتدي الخاتم في إصبعي دائمًا"

When they had eaten all the genie had brought, Aladdin sold one of the silver plates

عندما أكلوا كل ما أحضره الجني، باع علاء الدين أحد الأطباق الفضية

and when he needed money again he sold the next plate

وعندما احتاج إلى المال مرة أخرى باع اللوحة التالية

he did this until no plates were left

لقد فعل هذا حتى لم يبق أي طبق

He then made another wish to the genie

ثم قدم أمنية أخرى للجني

and the genie gave him another set of plates

وأعطاه الجني مجموعة أخرى من الأطباق

and in this way they lived for many years

وعلى هذا النحو عاشوا لسنوات عديدة

One day Aladdin heard an order from the Sultan

ذات يوم سمع علاء الدين أمراً من السلطان

everyone was to stay at home and close their shutters

كان على الجميع البقاء في المنزل وإغلاق مصاريعهم

the Princess was going to and from her bath

كانت الأميرة تذهب وتعود من حمامها

Aladdin was seized by a desire to see her face
لقد انتاب علاء الدين رغبة في رؤية وجهها
although it was very difficult to see her face
على الرغم من أنه كان من الصعب جدًا رؤية وجهها
because everywhere she went she wore a veil
لأنها كانت ترتدي الحجاب في كل مكان تذهب إليه
He hid himself behind the door of the bath
اختبأ خلف باب الحمام
and he peeped through a chink in the door
وألقى نظرة من خلال شق في الباب
The Princess lifted her veil as she went in to the bath
رفعت الأميرة حجابها عندما دخلت الحمام
and she looked so beautiful that Aladdin instantly fell in love with her
وبدت جميلة جدًا لدرجة أن علاء الدين وقع في حبها على الفور
He went home so changed that his mother was frightened
لقد عاد إلى المنزل وقد تغير كثيرًا لدرجة أن والدته كانت خائفة
He told her he loved the Princess so deeply that he could not live without her
أخبرها أنه يحب الأميرة بشدة لدرجة أنه لا يستطيع العيش بدونها
and he wanted to ask her in marriage of her father
وأراد أن يتقدم لخطبتها من أبيها
His mother, on hearing this, burst out laughing
انفجرت والدته ضاحكة عندما سمعت ذلك.
but Aladdin finally convinced her to go to the Sultan
لكن علاء الدين أقنعها في النهاية بالذهاب إلى السلطان
and she was going to carry his request
وكانت ستحمل طلبه
She fetched a napkin and laid in it the magic fruits
أحضرت منديلًا ووضعت فيه الفاكهة السحرية
the magic fruits from the enchanted garden
الفواكه السحرية من الحديقة المسحورة
the fruits sparkled and shone like the most beautiful jewels
كانت الثمار تتألق وتتألق مثل أجمل الجواهر
She took the magic fruits with her to please the Sultan
أخذت معها الفاكهة السحرية لإرضاء السلطان
and she set out, trusting in the lamp

وانطلقت وهي تثق في المصباح
The Grand Vizier and the lords of council had just gone into the palace
وكان الصدر الأعظم وأعضاء المجلس قد دخلوا القصر للتو
and she placed herself in front of the Sultan
ووضعت نفسها أمام السلطان
He, however, took no notice of her
ومع ذلك، لم ينتبه إليها
She went every day for a week
ذهبت كل يوم لمدة اسبوع
and she stood in the same place
ووقفت في نفس المكان
When the council broke up on the sixth day the Sultan said to his Vizier:
ولما انفض المجلس في اليوم السادس قال السلطان لوزيره :
"I see a certain woman in the audience-chamber every day"
"أرى امرأة معينة في قاعة الجمهور كل يوم "
"she is always carrying something in a napkin"
"إنها تحمل دائمًا شيئًا ما في منديل "
"Call her to come to us, next time"
"اتصل بها لتأتي إلينا في المرة القادمة "
"so that I may find out what she wants"
"لكي أتمكن من معرفة ما تريده "
Next day the Vizier gave her a sign
في اليوم التالي أعطاها الوزير إشارة
she went up to the foot of the throne
صعدت إلى أسفل العرش
and she remained kneeling till the Sultan spoke to her
وبقيت راكعة حتى كلمها السلطان .
"Rise, good woman, tell me what you want"
"قومي أيتها المرأة الصالحة، أخبريني ماذا تريدين "
She hesitated, so the Sultan sent away all but the Vizier
ترددت، فأرسل السلطان الجميع إلا الوزير .
and he bade her to speak frankly
وطلب منها أن تتحدث بصراحة
and he promised to forgive her for anything she might say

ووعدها بأن يسامحها على أي شيء قد تقوله

She then told him of her son's great love for the Princess

ثم أخبرته بحب ابنها الكبير للأميرة

"I prayed for him to forget her," she said

"لقد دعوت الله أن ينساها "قالت

"but my prayers were in vain"

"ولكن صلواتي ذهبت سدى"

"he threatened to do some desperate deed if I refused to go"

"لقد هددني بالقيام بعمل يائس إذا رفضت الذهاب"

"and so I ask your Majesty for the hand of the Princess"

"ولذلك أطلب من جلالتك يد الأميرة"

"but now I pray you to forgive me"

"ولكن الآن أطلب منك أن تسامحني"

"and I pray that you forgive my son Aladdin"

"و أرجو أن تسامح ابني علاء الدين"

The Sultan asked her kindly what she had in the napkin

فسألها السلطان بلطف ماذا يوجد في المنديل؟

so she unfolded the napkin

لذلك قامت بنشر المناديل

and she presented the jewels to the Sultan

وقدمت المجوهرات للسلطان

He was thunderstruck by the beauty of the jewels

لقد أذهل بجمال المجوهرات

and he turned to the Vizier and asked, "What sayest thou?"

والتفت إلى الوزير وسأله: ماذا تقول؟

"Ought I not to bestow the Princess on one who values her at such a price?"

"ألا ينبغي لي أن أمنح الأميرة لمن يقدرها بهذا الثمن؟"

The Vizier wanted her for his own son

أرادها الوزير لابنه

so he begged the Sultan to withhold her for three months

فطلب من السلطان أن يحجزها لمدة ثلاثة أشهر.

perhaps within the time his son would contrive to make a richer present

ربما في غضون الوقت الذي قد يتمكن فيه ابنه من صنع هدية أكثر ثراءً

The Sultan granted the wish of his Vizier

استجاب السلطان لرغبة وزيره
and he told Aladdin's mother that he consented to the marriage

وأخبر والدة علاء الدين أنه وافق على الزواج
but she was not allowed appear before him again for three months

ولكن لم يسمح لها بالمثول أمامه مرة أخرى لمدة ثلاثة أشهر .
Aladdin waited patiently for nearly three months

انتظر علاء الدين بصبر لمدة ثلاثة أشهر تقريبًا
after two months had elapsed his mother went to go to the market

بعد مرور شهرين ذهبت والدته إلى السوق
she was going into the city to buy oil

كانت ذاهبة إلى المدينة لشراء الزيت
when she got to the market she found every one rejoicing

عندما وصلت إلى السوق وجدت الجميع فرحين
so she asked what was going on

فسألت ماذا يحدث
"Do you not know?" was the answer

"هل لا تعلم؟" "كان الجواب
"the son of the Grand Vizier is to marry the Sultan's daughter tonight"

"ابن الصدر الأعظم سيتزوج ابنة السلطان الليلة "
Breathless, she ran and told Aladdin

وهي لاهثة الأنفاس، ركضت وأخبرت علاء الدين
at first Aladdin was overwhelmed

في البداية كان علاء الدين مندهشا
but then he thought of the magic lamp and rubbed it

ولكن بعد ذلك فكر في المصباح السحري وفركه
once again the genie appeared out of the lamp

مرة أخرى ظهر الجني من المصباح
"What is thy will?" asked the genie

"ما هي إرادتك؟ "سأل الجني
"The Sultan, as thou knowest, has broken his promise to me"

"إن السلطان كما تعلم قد أخلف وعده لي "
"the Vizier's son is to have the Princess"

"ابن الوزير سوف يحصل على الأميرة "

"My command is that tonight you bring the bride and bridegroom"

"أمري هو أن تحضروا الليلة العروس والعريس "

"Master, I obey," said the genie

"سيدي، أنا أطيع"، قال الجني

Aladdin then went to his chamber

ثم ذهب علاء الدين إلى غرفته

sure enough, at midnight the genie transported a bed

وبالفعل، في منتصف الليل، نقل الجني سريرًا

and the bed contained the Vizier's son and the Princess

وكان السرير يحتوي على ابن الوزير والأميرة

"Take this new-married man, genie," he said

"خذ هذا الرجل المتزوج حديثًا، أيها الجني"، قال

"put him outside in the cold for the night"

"ضعه خارجًا في البرد طوال الليل "

"then return the couple again at daybreak"

"ثم رجع الزوجان مرة أخرى عند الفجر "

So the genie took the Vizier's son out of bed

فأخرج الجني ابن الوزير من فراشه

and he left Aladdin with the Princess

وترك علاء الدين مع الأميرة

"Fear nothing," Aladdin said to her, "you are my wife"

"لا تخافي من شيء "قال لها علاء الدين" أنت زوجتي "

"you were promised to me by your unjust father"

"لقد وعدتني من قبل والدك الظالم "

"and no harm shall come to you"

"ولن يصيبكم سوء "

The Princess was too frightened to speak

كانت الأميرة خائفة جدًا من التحدث

and she passed the most miserable night of her life

وقضت أتعس ليلة في حياتها

although Aladdin lay down beside her and slept soundly

على الرغم من أن علاء الدين استلقى بجانبها ونام بعمق

At the appointed hour the genie fetched in the shivering bridegroom

في الساعة المحددة، أحضر الجني العريس المرتجف

he laid him in his place

وضعه في مكانه

and he transported the bed back to the palace

ونقل السرير إلى القصر

Presently the Sultan came to wish his daughter good-morning

وفي الحال جاء السلطان ليتمنى لابنته صباح الخير

The unhappy Vizier's son jumped up and hid himself

قفز ابن الوزير الحزين واختبأ

and the Princess would not say a word

والأميرة لم تقل كلمة واحدة

and she was very sorrowful

وكانت حزينة جدا

The Sultan sent her mother to her

أرسل السلطان أمها إليها

"Why will you not speak to your father, child?"

"لماذا لا تتحدث مع والدك يا ابني؟"

"What has happened?" she asked

"ماذا حدث؟" سألت

The Princess sighed deeply

تنهدت الأميرة بعمق

and at last she told her mother what had happened

وأخيرا أخبرت أمها بما حدث

she told her how the bed had been carried into some strange house

أخبرتها كيف تم نقل السرير إلى منزل غريب

and she told of what had happened in the house

وأخبرت بما حدث في البيت

Her mother did not believe her in the least

لم تصدقها والدتها على الإطلاق

and she bade her to consider it an idle dream

وطلبت منها أن تعتبره حلما فارغا

The following night exactly the same thing happened

وفي الليلة التالية حدث نفس الشيء بالضبط

and the next morning the princess wouldn't speak either

وفي الصباح التالي لم تتحدث الأميرة أيضًا

on the Princess's refusal to speak, the Sultan threatened to cut off her head

وعند رفض الأميرة الحديث هددها السلطان بقطع رأسها

She then confessed all that had happened

ثم اعترفت بكل ما حدث

and she bid him to ask the Vizier's son

وأمرته أن يسأل ابن الوزير

The Sultan told the Vizier to ask his son

فقال السلطان للوزير أن يسأل ابنه

and the Vizier's son told the truth

فقال ابن الوزير الحقيقة

he added that he dearly loved the Princess

وأضاف أنه أحب الأميرة كثيرًا

"but I would rather die than go through another such fearful night"

"لكنني أفضل أن أموت على أن أعيش ليلة أخرى مخيفة كهذه "

and he wished to be separated from her, which was granted

وأراد أن ينفصل عنها، فتم ذلك .

and then there was an end to the feasting and rejoicing

وبعد ذلك انتهى الاحتفال والابتهاج

then the three months were over

ثم انتهت الثلاثة أشهر

Aladdin sent his mother to remind the Sultan of his promise

أرسل علاء الدين أمه لتذكير السلطان بوعده

She stood in the same place as before

وقفت في نفس المكان كما كان من قبل

the Sultan had forgotten Aladdin

لقد نسي السلطان علاء الدين

but at once he remembered him again

ولكنه تذكره مرة أخرى على الفور

and he asked for her to come to him

وطلب منها أن تأتي إليه

On seeing her poverty the Sultan felt less inclined than ever to keep his word

عندما رأى السلطان فقرها، شعر بأنه أقل ميلاً من أي وقت مضى إلى الوفاء بوعده .

and he asked his Vizier's advice

وطلب نصيحة وزيره

he counselled him to set a high value on the Princess
نصحه بوضع قيمة عالية للأميرة
a price so high that no man alive could come afford her
سعر مرتفع للغاية بحيث لا يستطيع أي رجل على قيد الحياة أن يتحمله
The Sultan then turned to Aladdin's mother, saying:
ثم التفت السلطان إلى أم علاء الدين قائلاً :
"Good woman, a Sultan must remember his promises"
"المرأة الصالحة، يجب على السلطان أن يتذكر وعوده "
"and I will remember my promise"
"وسوف أتذكر وعدي "
"but your son must first send me forty basins of gold"
"ولكن يجب على ابنك أن يرسل لي أولاً أربعين حوضًا من الذهب "
"and the gold basins must be full of jewels"
"ويجب أن تكون الأحواض الذهبية مليئة بالجواهر "
"and they must be carried by forty black camels"
"ويجب أن تحملها أربعون بعيرًا سوداء "
"and in front of each black camel there is to be a white camel"
"و أمام كل جمل أسود جمل أبيض "
"and all the camels are to be splendidly dressed"
"ويجب أن تكون جميع الإبل مزينة بشكل رائع "
"Tell him that I await his answer"
"أخبره أنني أنتظر جوابه "
The mother of Aladdin bowed low
انحنت أم علاء الدين
and then she went home
ثم ذهبت إلى منزلها
although she thought all was lost
على الرغم من أنها اعتقدت أن كل شيء قد ضاع
She gave Aladdin the message
لقد أعطت علاء الدين الرسالة
and she added, "He may wait long enough for your answer!"
وأضافت: "قد ينتظر وقتًا طويلاً للحصول على إجابتك" !
"Not so long as you think, mother," her son replied
"ليس كما تعتقدين يا أمي" أجابها ابنها
"I would do a great deal more than that for the Princess"

"سأفعل أكثر من ذلك بكثير للأميرة "
and he summoned the genie again
واستدعى الجني مرة أخرى
and in a few moments the eighty camels arrived
وفي لحظات وصلت الثمانون جملا
and they took up all space in the small house and garden
واحتلوا كل المساحة في البيت الصغير والحديقة
Aladdin made the camels set out to the palace
أرسل علاء الدين الجمال إلى القصر
and the camels were followed by his mother
وكانت الإبل تتبعه أمه
The camels were very richly dressed
كانت الإبل ترتدي ملابس غنية جدًا
and splendid jewels were on the girdles of the camels
وكانت الجواهر الرائعة على أحزمة الإبل
and everyone crowded around to see the camels
وتزاحم الجميع حول الإبل لرؤية
and they saw the basins of gold the camels carried on their backs
ورأوا أحواض الذهب التي تحملها الإبل على ظهورها
They entered the palace of the Sultan
دخلوا قصر السلطان
and the camels kneeled before him in a semi circle
وركعت الإبل أمامه في شكل نصف دائرة .
and Aladdin's mother presented the camels to the Sultan
وأهدت أم علاء الدين الإبل إلى السلطان
He hesitated no longer, but said:
ولم يتردد أكثر من ذلك، بل قال :
"Good woman, return to your son"
"أيتها المرأة الصالحة ارجعي إلى ابنك "
"tell him that I wait for him with open arms"
"أخبره أنني أنتظره بذراعين مفتوحتين "
She lost no time in telling Aladdin
لم تضيع أي وقت في إخبار علاء الدين
and she bid him to make haste
وطلبت منه أن يسرع

But Aladdin first called for the genie
لكن علاء الدين نادى على الجني أولاً

"I want a scented bath," he said
"أريد حمامًا معطرًا "قال

"and I want a horse more beautiful than the Sultan's"
"وأريد حصانا أجمل من حصان السلطان "

"and I want twenty servants to attend to me"
"وأريد عشرين خادمًا لخدمتي "

"and I also want six beautifully dressed servants to wait on my mother"
"وأريد أيضًا ستة خدم يرتدون ملابس جميلة لخدمة والدتي "

"and lastly, I want ten thousand pieces of gold in ten purses"
"وأخيرًا، أريد عشرة آلاف قطعة من الذهب في عشرة محافظ "

No sooner had he said what he wanted and it was done
لم يكد يقول ما يريده حتى تم ذلك

Aladdin mounted his beautiful horse
ركب علاء الدين حصانه الجميل

and he passed through the streets
ومرّ عبر الشوارع

the servants cast gold into the crowd as they went
ألقى الخدم الذهب على الجمع وهم ذاهبون

Those who had played with him in his childhood knew him not
الذين لعبوا معه في طفولته لم يعرفوه

he had grown very handsome
لقد أصبح وسيمًا جدًا

When the Sultan saw him he came down from his throne
فلما رآه السلطان نزل عن عرشه

he embraced his new son-in-law with open arms
احتضن صهره الجديد بذراعين مفتوحتين

and he led him into a hall where a feast was spread
وأدخله إلى قاعة حيث أقيمت وليمة .

he intended to marry him to the Princess that very day
كان ينوي أن يزوجه للأميرة في نفس اليوم

But Aladdin refused to marry straight away
لكن علاء الدين رفض الزواج على الفور

"first I must build a palace fit for the princess"

"أولاً يجب أن أبني قصرًا يليق بالأميرة "

and then he took his leave

ثم أخذ إجازته

Once home, he said to the genie:

وعندما وصل إلى منزله، قال للجني :

"Build me a palace of the finest marble"

"ابني لي قصرًا من أجود أنواع الرخام "

"set the palace with jasper, agate, and other precious stones"

"زخرف القصر باليشب والعقيق والأحجار الكريمة الأخرى "

"In the middle of the palace you shall build me a large hall with a dome"

"في وسط القصر ستبني لي قاعة كبيرة ذات قبة "

"the four walls of the hall will be of masses of gold and silver"

"ستكون الجدران الأربعة للقاعة من كتل من الذهب والفضة "

"and each wall will have six windows"

"وكل حائط فيه ستة شبابيك "

"and the lattices of the windows will be set with precious jewels"

"وسوف تُرصَّع شباك النوافذ بالجواهر الثمينة "

"but there must be one window that is not decorated"

"ولكن يجب أن تكون هناك نافذة واحدة غير مزخرفة "

"go see that it gets done!"

"اذهب وتأكد من إنجاز الأمر "!

The palace was finished by the next day

تم الانتهاء من القصر في اليوم التالي

the genie carried him to the new palace

حمله الجني إلى القصر الجديد

and he showed him how all his orders had been faithfully carried out

وأظهر له كيف تم تنفيذ جميع أوامره بأمانة .

even a velvet carpet had been laid from Aladdin's palace to the Sultan's

حتى أن سجادة مخملية تم وضعها من قصر علاء الدين إلى قصر السلطان .

Aladdin's mother then dressed herself carefully

ثم ارتدت والدة علاء الدين ملابسها بعناية

and she walked to the palace with her servants
وذهبت إلى القصر مع خدمها
and Aladdin followed her on horseback
وتبعها علاء الدين على ظهر الحصان
The Sultan sent musicians with trumpets and cymbals to meet them
فأرسل السلطان موسيقيين بالأبواق والصنوج لاستقبالهم
so the air resounded with music and cheers
فكان الهواء ملينا بالموسيقى والهتافات
She was taken to the Princess, who saluted her
تم اصطحابها إلى الأميرة التي سلمت عليها
and she treated her with great honour
وعاملتها بكل احترام
At night the Princess said good-bye to her father
وفي الليل ودعت الأميرة والدها
and she set out on the carpet for Aladdin's palace
وانطلقت على السجادة إلى قصر علاء الدين
his mother was at her side
كانت أمها بجانبها
and they were followed by their entourage of servants
وتبعهم حاشيتهم من الخدم
She was charmed at the sight of Aladdin
لقد سُحِرت برؤية علاء الدين
and Aladdin ran to receive her into the palace
وركض علاء الدين لاستقبالها في القصر
"Princess," he said, "blame your beauty for my boldness"
"قال،"" يا أميرة، ألوم جمالك على جرأتي """"
"I hope I have not displeased you"
"أتمنى أن لا أكون قد أغضبتك "
she said she willingly obeyed her father in this matter
قالت إنها أطاعت والدها في هذا الأمر طوعا
because she had seen that he is handsome
لأنها رأت أنه وسيم
After the wedding had taken place Aladdin led her into the hall
بعد أن تم الزفاف، أخذها علاء الدين إلى القاعة
a great feast was spread out in the hall

أقيم وليمة عظيمة في القاعة

and she supped with him

وتعشيت معه

after eating they danced till midnight

بعد الأكل رقصوا حتى منتصف الليل

The next day Aladdin invited the Sultan to see the palace

وفي اليوم التالي دعا علاء الدين السلطان لرؤية القصر

they entered the hall with the four-and-twenty windows

دخلوا القاعة ذات النوافذ الأربع والعشرين

the windows were decorated with rubies, diamonds, and emeralds

تم تزيين النوافذ بالياقوت والماس والزمرد

he cried, "The palace is one of the wonders of the world!"

فصاح قائلا : هذا القصر من عجائب الدنيا !

"There is only one thing that surprises me"

"هناك شيء واحد فقط يفاجئني "

"Was it by accident that one window was left unfinished?"

"هل كان من قبيل الصدفة أن تُركت إحدى النوافذ غير مكتملة ؟ "

"No, sir, it was done so by design," replied Aladdin

"لا سيدي، لقد تم ذلك عن قصد"، أجاب علاء الدين

"I wished your Majesty to have the glory of finishing this palace"

"تمنيت لجلالتك أن تحظى بشرف الانتهاء من هذا القصر "

The Sultan was pleased to be given this honour

وقد سر السلطان أن يحظى بهذا التكريم

and he sent for the best jewellers in the city

وأرسل في طلب أفضل الصاغة في المدينة .

He showed them the unfinished window

أظهر لهم النافذة غير المكتملة

and he bade them to decorate the window like the others

وأمرهم بتزيين النافذة مثل الآخرين

"Sir," replied their spokesman

أجاب المتحدث باسمهم" :سيدي . "

"we cannot find enough jewels"

"لا يمكننا العثور على ما يكفي من المجوهرات "

so the Sultan had his own jewels fetched

لذلك قام السلطان بإحضار جواهره الخاصة

but those jewels were soon used up too

ولكن تلك الجواهر استنفدت أيضا قريبا

even after a month's time the work was not half done

حتى بعد مرور شهر لم يتم الانتهاء من نصف العمل

Aladdin knew that their task was impossible

عرف علاء الدين أن مهمتهم مستحيلة

he bade them to undo their work

وأمرهم بالتراجع عن عملهم

and he bade them to carry the jewels back

وأمرهم بحمل الجواهر

the genie finished the window at his command

انتهى الجني من النافذة بأمره

The Sultan was surprised to receive his jewels again

تفاجأ السلطان بحصوله على جواهره مرة أخرى

he visited Aladdin, who showed him the finished window

زار علاء الدين الذي أظهر له النافذة النهائية

and the Sultan embraced his son in law

واحتضن السلطان صهره

meanwhile, the envious Vizier suspected the work of enchantment

وفي هذه الأثناء، شك الوزير الحسود في عمل السحر .

Aladdin had won the hearts of the people by his gentle manner

لقد فاز علاء الدين بقلوب الناس بأسلوبه اللطيف

He was made captain of the Sultan's armies

تم تعيينه قائدا لجيوش السلطان

and he won several battles for his army

وفاز بعدة معارك لجيشه

but he remained as modest and courteous as before

لكنه ظل متواضعا ومهذبا كما كان من قبل

in this way he lived in peace and content for several years

بهذه الطريقة عاش في سلام ورضا لعدة سنوات

But far away in Africa the magician remembered Aladdin

ولكن في مكان بعيد في أفريقيا، تذكر الساحر علاء الدين .

and by his magic arts he discovered Aladdin hadn't perished in the cave

وباستخدام فنونه السحرية اكتشف أن علاء الدين لم يهلك في الكهف .

but instead of perishing, he had escaped and married the princess

ولكن بدلاً من الهلاك، هرب وتزوج الأميرة .

and now he was living in great honour and wealth

وكان الآن يعيش في شرف عظيم وثروة

He knew that the poor tailor's son could only have accomplished this by means of the magic lamp

لقد كان يعلم أن ابن الخياط الفقير لم يكن ليتمكن من تحقيق ذلك إلا باستخدام المصباح السحري .

and he travelled night and day until he reached the city

وسافر ليلًا ونهارًا حتى وصل إلى المدينة

he was bent on making sure of Aladdin's ruin

كان عازمًا على التأكد من تدمير علاء الدين

As he passed through the town he heard people talking

وبينما كان يمر بالمدينة سمع الناس يتحدثون

all they could talk about was the marvellous palace

كل ما استطاعوا التحدث عنه هو القصر الرائع

"Forgive my ignorance," he asked

"اغفر لي جهلي "سأل

"what is this palace you speak of?"

" ما هو هذا القصر الذي تتحدث عنه؟ "

"Have you not heard of Prince Aladdin's palace?" was the reply

"ألم تسمع عن قصر الأمير علاء الدين؟ "كان الرد

"the palace is one of the greatest wonders of the world"

"يعتبر القصر من أعظم عجائب الدنيا "

"I will direct you to the palace, if you would like to see it"

"سأرشدك إلى القصر إذا كنت ترغب في رؤيته "

The magician thanked him for bringing him to the palace

شكره الساحر على إحضاره إلى القصر

and having seen the palace, he knew that it had been built by the Genie of the Lamp

ولما رأى القصر عرف أنه قد بناه جني المصباح

this made him half mad with rage

هذا جعله نصف مجنون من الغضب

He was determined to get hold of the magic lamp

كان مصمما على الحصول على المصباح السحري

and he was going to plunge Aladdin into the deepest poverty again

وكان على وشك أن يغرق علاء الدين في أعمق فقر مرة أخرى

Unluckily, Aladdin had gone on a hunting trip for eight days

لسوء الحظ، ذهب علاء الدين في رحلة صيد لمدة ثمانية أيام

this gave the magician plenty of time

وهذا أعطى الساحر الكثير من الوقت

He bought a dozen copper lamps

اشترى عشرة مصابيح نحاسية

and he put the copper lamps into a basket

ووضع المصابيح النحاسية في سلة

and then he went to the palace

ثم ذهب إلى القصر

"New lamps for old lamps!" he exclaimed

"مصابيح جديدة للمصابيح القديمة" إصاح

and he was followed by a jeering crowd

وتبعه حشد من الساخرين

The Princess was sitting in the hall of four-and-twenty windows

كانت الأميرة جالسة في قاعة ذات أربع وعشرين نافذة

she sent a servant to find out what the noise was about

أرسلت خادمًا لمعرفة سبب الضجيج

the servant came back laughing so much that the Princess scolded her

عادت الخادمة وهي تضحك كثيرا حتى أن الأميرة وبختها

"Madam," replied the servant

"سيدتي" أجاب الخادم

"who can help but laughing when you see such a thing?"

"من يستطيع أن لا يضحك عندما يرى مثل هذا الشيء؟"

"an old fool is offering to exchange fine new lamps for old lamps"

"يعرض رجل عجوز أحمق استبدال المصابيح الجديدة الجميلة بالمصابيح القديمة"

Another servant, hearing this, spoke up

فسمع خادم آخر هذا فتكلم

"There is an old lamp on the cornice which he can have"
"يوجد مصباح قديم على الكورنيش يمكنه الحصول عليه"
this, of course, was the magic lamp
هذا، بالطبع، كان المصباح السحري
Aladdin had left the magic lamp there, as he could not take it with him
لقد ترك علاء الدين المصباح السحري هناك، لأنه لم يستطع أن يأخذه معه .
The Princess didn't know know the lamp's value
الأميرة لم تعرف قيمة المصباح
laughingly, she bade the servant to exchange the magic lamp
ضاحكة، طلبت من الخادمة أن تستبدل المصباح السحري .
the servant took the lamp to the magician
أخذ الخادم المصباح إلى الساحر
"Give me a new lamp for this lamp," she said
"أعطني مصباحًا جديدًا لهذا المصباح "قالت
He snatched the lamp and bade the servant to pick another lamp
انتزع المصباح وطلب من الخادم أن يختار مصباحًا آخر
and the entire crowd jeered at the sight
وسخر الحشد بأكمله من المشهد
but the magician cared little for the crowd
لكن الساحر لم يهتم بالحشد
he left the crowd with the magic lamp he had set out to get
غادر الحشد بالمصباح السحري الذي كان قد شرع في إحضاره
and he went out of the city gates to a lonely place
وخرج من أبواب المدينة إلى مكان قفر .
there he remained till nightfall
وبقي هناك حتى حلول الليل
and at nightfall he pulled out the magic lamp and rubbed it
وعند حلول الليل أخرج المصباح السحري وفركه
The genie appeared to the magician
ظهر الجني للساحر
and the magician made his command to the genie
وأصدر الساحر أمره إلى الجني
"carry me, the princess, and the palace to a lonely place in Africa"

"احملوني، أنا الأميرة، والقصر إلى مكان منعزل في أفريقيا "

Next morning the Sultan looked out of the window toward Aladdin's palace

وفي صباح اليوم التالي نظر السلطان من النافذة نحو قصر علاء الدين

and he rubbed his eyes when he saw the palace was gone

وفرك عينيه عندما رأى أن القصر قد اختفى

He sent for the Vizier and asked what had become of the palace

فأرسل إلى الوزير وسأله عما حدث للقصر

The Vizier looked out too, and was lost in astonishment

ونظر الوزير أيضًا، فذهل من هول ما رأى .

He again put the events down to enchantment

لقد أرجع الأحداث مرة أخرى إلى السحر

and this time the Sultan believed him

وهذه المرة صدقه السلطان

he sent thirty men on horseback to fetch Aladdin in chains

أرسل ثلاثين رجلاً على ظهور الخيل لإحضار علاء الدين مقيدًا بالسلاسل

They met him riding home

لقد التقوا به وهو راكبا إلى المنزل

they bound him and forced him to go with them on foot

قيدوه وأجبروه على الذهاب معهم سيرًا على الأقدام

The people, however, who loved him, followed them to the palace

أما الناس الذين أحبوه فقد تبعوهم إلى القصر

they would make sure that he came to no harm

سوف يتأكدون من أنه لم يتعرض لأذى

He was carried before the Sultan

تم حمله أمام السلطان

and the Sultan ordered the executioner to cut off his head

وأمر السلطان الجلاد بقطع رأسه .

The executioner made Aladdin kneel down before a block of wood

جعل الجلاد علاء الدين يركع أمام كتلة من الخشب

he bandaged his eyes so that he could not see

لقد ضمد عينيه حتى لا يتمكن من الرؤية

and he raised his scimitar to strike

ورفع سيفه ليضرب

At that instant the Vizier saw the crowd had forced their way into the courtyard

وفي تلك اللحظة رأى الوزير أن الحشد قد اقتحم الفناء .

they were scaling the walls to rescue Aladdin

كانوا يتسلقون الجدران لإنقاذ علاء الدين

so he called to the executioner to halt

فنادى على الجلاد أن يتوقف

The people, indeed, looked so threatening that the Sultan gave way

لقد بدا الناس في الواقع مخيفين للغاية لدرجة أن السلطان استسلم .

and he ordered Aladdin to be unbound

وأمر علاء الدين بأن يُطلق سراحه

he pardoned him in the sight of the crowd

عفا عنه أمام الحشد

Aladdin now begged to know what he had done

توسل علاء الدين الآن لمعرفة ما فعله

"False wretch!" said the Sultan, "come thither"

"أيها الوغد الكاذب، تعال إلى هناك "إقال السلطان .

he showed him from the window the place where his palace had stood

أظهر له من النافذة المكان الذي كان يقع فيه قصره

Aladdin was so amazed that he could not say a word

لقد اندهش علاء الدين لدرجة أنه لم يستطع أن يقول كلمة واحدة

"Where are my palace and my daughter?" demanded the Sultan

"أين قصري وابنتي؟ "سأل السلطان .

"For the palace I am not so deeply concerned"

"بالنسبة للقصر، أنا لست قلقًا للغاية "

"but my daughter I must have"

"لكن ابنتي يجب أن أحصل عليها "

"and you must find her, or lose your head"

"ويجب عليك أن تجدها، أو تفقد رأسك "

Aladdin begged to be granted forty days in which to find her

توسل علاء الدين أن يمنحه مهلة أربعين يومًا للعثور عليها .

he promised that if he failed he would return

وعد أنه إذا فشل فسوف يعود

and on his return he would suffer death at the Sultan's pleasure

وعند عودته كان يموت بناء على رغبة السلطان .

His prayer was granted by the Sultan

استجاب له السلطان

and he went forth sadly from the Sultan's presence

وخرج حزينا من عند السلطان

For three days he wandered about like a madman

لمدة ثلاثة أيام كان يتجول كالمجنون

he asked everyone what had become of his palace

سأل الجميع عما حدث لقصره

but they only laughed and pitied him

لكنهم فقط ضحكوا عليه وأشفقوا عليه

He came to the banks of a river

وصل إلى ضفاف النهر

he knelt down to say his prayers before throwing himself in

ركع ليقول صلاته قبل أن يلقي بنفسه في

In so doing he rubbed the magic ring he still wore

وبذلك قام بفرك الخاتم السحري الذي كان لا يزال يرتديه

The genie he had seen in the cave appeared

ظهر الجني الذي رآه في الكهف

and he asked him what his will was

فسأله ما هي وصيته

"Save my life, genie," said Aladdin

"أنقذ حياتي أيها الجني "قال علاء الدين

"bring my palace back"

" أعيدوا لي قصري "

"That is not in my power," said the genie

"هذا ليس في قدرتي "قال الجني

"I am only the Slave of the Ring"

"أنا مجرد عبد الخاتم "

"you must ask him for the magic lamp"

"يجب أن تطلب منه المصباح السحري "

"that might be true," said Aladdin

"قد يكون هذا صحيحا "قال علاء الدين

"but thou canst take me to the palace"

"ولكن يمكنك أن تأخذني إلى القصر "
"set me down under my dear wife's window"
"ضعني تحت نافذة زوجتي العزيزة "

He at once found himself in Africa
لقد وجد نفسه على الفور في أفريقيا

he was under the window of the Princess
كان تحت نافذة الأميرة

and he fell asleep out of sheer weariness
ونام من شدة التعب

He was awakened by the singing of the birds
لقد استيقظ على غناء الطيور

and his heart was lighter than it was before
وكان قلبه أخف مما كان عليه من قبل

He saw that all his misfortunes were due to the loss of the magic lamp
رأى أن كل مصائبه كانت بسبب فقدان المصباح السحري

and he vainly wondered who had robbed him of his magic lamp
وتساءل عبثًا عمن سرق منه مصباحه السحري

That morning the Princess rose earlier than she normally
في ذلك الصباح استيقظت الأميرة مبكرًا عن المعتاد

once a day she was forced to endure the magicians company
مرة واحدة في اليوم كانت مجبرة على تحمل صحبة السحرة

She, however, treated him very harshly
لكنها تعامله بقسوة شديدة

so he dared not live with her in the palace
لذلك لم يجرؤ على العيش معها في القصر

As she was dressing, one of her women looked out and saw Aladdin
وبينما كانت ترتدي ملابسها، نظرت إحدى نسائها إلى الخارج ورأت علاء الدين

The Princess ran and opened the window
ركضت الأميرة وفتحت النافذة

at the noise she made Aladdin looked up
عند الضجيج الذي أحدثته نظر علاء الدين إلى الأعلى

She called to him to come to her

نادت عليه ليأتي إليها
it was a great joy for the lovers to see each other again
لقد كان من دواعي سرور العشاق أن يروا بعضهم البعض مرة أخرى
After he had kissed her Aladdin said:
وبعد أن قبلها قال علاء الدين :
"I beg of you, Princess, in God's name"
"أتوسل إليك يا أميرتي باسم الله"
"before we speak of anything else"
"قبل أن نتحدث عن أي شيء آخر"
"for your own sake and mine"
"من أجل مصلحتك ومصلحتي"
"tell me what has become of the old lamp"
"أخبرني ماذا حدث للمصباح القديم"
"I left the lamp on the cornice in the hall of four-and-twenty windows"
"تركت المصباح على الكورنيش في قاعة الأربع والعشرين نافذة"
"Alas!" she said, "I am the innocent cause of our sorrows"
قالت" آه، أنا السبب البريء في أحزاننا"
and she told him of the exchange of the magic lamp
وأخبرته عن تبادل المصباح السحري
"Now I know," cried Aladdin
"الآن عرفت" صرخ علاء الدين
"we have to thank the magician for this!"
"علينا أن نشكر الساحر على هذا"!
"Where is the magic lamp?"
"أين المصباح السحري؟"
"He carries the lamp about with him," said the Princess
"إنه يحمل المصباح معه"، قالت الأميرة
"I know he carries the lamp with him"
"أعلم أنه يحمل المصباح معه"
"because he pulled the lamp out of his breast pocket to show me"
"لأنه أخرج المصباح من جيب صدره ليظهر لي"
"and he wishes me to break my faith with you and marry him"
"وهو يريد مني أن أخالف وعدي معك وأتزوجه"
"and he said you were beheaded by my father's command"

"وقال لقد قطعت رأسك بأمر أبي "
"He is always speaking ill of you"
"إنه يتحدث عنك دائمًا بالسوء "
"but I only reply with my tears"
"ولكنني لا أرد إلا بدموعي "
"If I can persist, I doubt not"
"إذا كان بإمكاني المثابرة، فلا شك في ذلك "
"but he will use violence"
"لكنه سوف يستخدم العنف "
Aladdin comforted his wife
علاء الدين يواسي زوجته
and he left her for a while
وتركها لفترة من الوقت
He changed clothes with the first person he met in town
قام بتبديل ملابسه مع أول شخص قابله في المدينة
and having bought a certain powder, he returned to the Princess
وبعد أن اشترى مسحوقًا معينًا، عاد إلى الأميرة
the Princess let him in by a little side door
سمحت له الأميرة بالدخول من باب جانبي صغير
"Put on your most beautiful dress," he said to her
"ارتدي أجمل ما عندك "قال لها
"receive the magician with smiles today"
"استقبل الساحر بالابتسامات اليوم "
"lead him to believe that you have forgotten me"
"أجعله يعتقد أنك نسيتني "
"Invite him to sup with you"
"ادعوه لتناول العشاء معك "
"and tell him you wish to taste the wine of his country"
"وأخبره أنك ترغب في تذوق نبيذ بلاده "
"He will be gone for some time"
"سيكون رحل لبعض الوقت "
"while he is gone I will tell you what to do"
"أثناء غيابه سأخبرك بما يجب عليك فعله "
She listened carefully to Aladdin
لقد استمعت بعناية إلى علاء الدين

and when he left she arrayed herself beautifully
وعندما غادرت زينت نفسها بشكل جميل
she hadn't dressed like this since she had left her city
لم ترتدي مثل هذه الملابس منذ أن غادرت مدينتها
She put on a girdle and head-dress of diamonds
وضعت على رأسها حزامًا وغطاء رأس من الماس
she was more beautiful than ever
لقد كانت أكثر جمالا من أي وقت مضى
and she received the magician with a smile
واستقبلت الساحر بابتسامة
"I have made up my mind that Aladdin is dead"
"لقد قررت أن علاء الدين مات "
"my tears will not bring him back to me"
"دموعي لن تعيده لي "
"so I am resolved to mourn no more"
"لذا قررت أن لا أحزن بعد الآن "
"therefore I invite you to sup with me"
"لذلك أدعوك لتناول العشاء معي "
"but I am tired of the wines we have"
"لكنني تعبت من النبيذ الذي لدينا "
"I would like to taste the wines of Africa"
"أود أن أتذوق نبيذ أفريقيا "
The magician ran to his cellar
ركض الساحر إلى قبوه
and the Princess put the powder Aladdin had given her in her cup
ووضعت الأميرة المسحوق الذي أعطاه لها علاء الدين في كوبها
When he returned she asked him to drink to her health
عندما عاد طلبت منه أن يشرب لصحتها
and she handed him her cup in exchange for his
وأعطته كأسها مقابل ذلك .
this was done as a sign to show she was reconciled to him
لقد تم ذلك كعلامة على أنها تصالحت معه
Before drinking the magician made her a speech
قبل أن تشرب الساحره ألقت عليها خطابا
he wanted to praise her beauty

أراد أن يمدح جمالها

but the Princess cut him short

لكن الأميرة قطعته

"Let us drink first"

"دعونا نشرب أولا"

"and you shall say what you will afterwards"

"وأنت تقول ما تريد بعد ذلك"

She set her cup to her lips and kept it there

وضعت كأسها على شفتيها وأبقته هناك

the magician drained his cup to the dregs

لقد استنزف الساحر كأسه حتى الثمالة

and upon finishing his drink he fell back lifeless

وبعد أن انتهى من شرابه سقط على ظهره بلا حراك

The Princess then opened the door to Aladdin

ثم فتحت الأميرة الباب لعلاء الدين

and she flung her arms round his neck

وألقت ذراعيها حول عنقه

but Aladdin asked her to leave him

لكن علاء الدين طلب منها أن تتركه

there was still more to be done

لا يزال هناك المزيد الذي يتعين القيام به

He then went to the dead magician

ثم ذهب إلى الساحر الميت

and he took the lamp out of his vest

وأخرج المصباح من صدره

he bade the genie to carry the palace back

أمر الجني بحمل القصر مرة أخرى

the Princess in her chamber only felt two little shocks

لم تشعر الأميرة في غرفتها إلا بصدمتين صغيرتين

in little time she was at home again

في وقت قصير كانت في المنزل مرة أخرى

The Sultan was sitting on his balcony

وكان السلطان جالسا على شرفته

he was mourning for his lost daughter

كان حزينا على ابنته المفقودة

he looked up and had to rub his eyes again

نظر إلى الأعلى واضطر إلى فرك عينيه مرة أخرى

the palace stood there as it had before

كان القصر قائما هناك كما كان من قبل

He hastened over to the palace to see his daughter

أسرع إلى القصر ليرى ابنته

Aladdin received him in the hall of the palace

استقبله علاء الدين في قاعة القصر

and the princess was at his side

وكانت الأميرة بجانبه

Aladdin told him what had happened

أخبره علاء الدين بما حدث

and he showed him the dead body of the magician

فأراه جثة الساحر

so that the Sultan would believe him

حتى يصدقه السلطان

A ten days' feast was proclaimed

تم إعلان عيد لمدة عشرة أيام

and it seemed as if Aladdin might now live the rest of his life in peace

وبدا الأمر وكأن علاء الدين قد يعيش الآن بقية حياته في سلام .

but his life was not to be as peaceful as he had hoped

لكن حياته لم تكن هادئة كما كان يأمل

The African magician had a younger brother

كان للساحر الأفريقي أخ أصغر منه

he was maybe even more wicked and cunning than his brother

ربما كان أكثر شرًا ومكرًا من أخيه

He travelled to Aladdin to avenge his brother's death

سافر إلى علاء الدين للانتقام لموت أخيه

he went to visit a pious woman called Fatima

ذهب لزيارة امرأة صالحة اسمها فاطمة

he thought she might be of use to him

اعتقد أنها قد تكون مفيدة له

He entered her cell and put a dagger to her breast

دخل زنزانتها ووضع خنجرا في صدرها

then he told her to rise and do his bidding

ثم طلب منها أن تنهض وتنفذ أمره
and if she didn't he said he would kill her
وإذا لم تفعل ذلك قال أنه سيقتلها
He changed his clothes with her
لقد غير ملابسه معها
and he coloured his face like hers
وصبغ وجهه مثل وجهها
he put on her veil so that he looked just like her
وضع عليها الحجاب حتى أصبح يشبهها تماما
and finally he murdered her despite her compliance
وأخيرا قتلها رغم امتثالها
so that she could tell no tales
حتى لا تتمكن من سرد أي حكايات
Then he went towards the palace of Aladdin
ثم ذهب نحو قصر علاء الدين
all the people thought he was the holy woman
كان كل الناس يعتقدون أنه المرأة المقدسة
they gathered round him to kiss his hands
اجتمعوا حوله لتقبيل يديه
and they begged for his blessing
وطلبوا بركاته
When he got to the palace there was a great commotion around him
عندما وصل إلى القصر كان هناك ضجة كبيرة حوله
the princess wanted to know what all the noise was about
أرادت الأميرة أن تعرف سبب كل هذا الضجيج
so she bade her servant to look out of the window
لذلك طلبت من خادمتها أن تنظر من النافذة
and her servant asked what the noise was all about
وسألها خادمها عن سبب كل هذا الضجيج
she found out it was the holy woman causing the commotion
اكتشفت أن المرأة المقدسة هي التي تسببت في هذا الاضطراب
she was curing people of their ailments by touching them
كانت تشفي الناس من أمراضهم عن طريق لمسها
the Princess had long desired to see Fatima
كانت الأميرة ترغب منذ فترة طويلة في رؤية فاطمة

so she got her servant to ask her into the palace

لذلك طلبت من خادمها أن يدعوها إلى القصر

and the false Fatima accepted the offer into the palace

وقبلت فاطمة الكاذبة العرض بالدخول إلى القصر

the magician offered up a prayer for her health and prosperity

قدم الساحر صلاة من أجل صحتها وازدهارها

the Princess made him sit by her

جعلته الأميرة يجلس بجانبها

and she begged him to stay with her

وتوسلت إليه أن يبقى معها

The false Fatima wished for nothing better

لم تتمنى فاطمة الكاذبة شيئا أفضل

and she consented to the princess' wish

ووافقت على رغبة الأميرة

but he kept his veil down

ولكنه أبقى حجابه منخفضا

because he knew that he would be discovered otherwise

لأنه كان يعلم أنه سيتم اكتشافه بخلاف ذلك

The Princess showed him the hall

أظهرت له الأميرة القاعة

and she asked him what he thought of the hall

وسألته ما رأيه في القاعة

"It is a truly beautiful hall," said the false Fatima

"إنها قاعة جميلة حقًّا"، قالت فاطمة الكاذبة

"but in my mind your palace still wants one thing"

"لكن في ذهني قصرك لا يزال يريد شيئًا واحدًا "

"And what is it that my palace is missing?" asked the Princess

"وماذا ينقص قصري؟ "سألت الأميرة

"If only a Roc's egg were hung up from the middle of this dome"

"لو تم تعليق بيضة روك في منتصف هذه القبة "

"then your palace would be the wonder of the world," he said

"ثم سيكون قصرك من عجائب الدنيا "قال

After this the Princess could think of nothing but the Roc's egg

بعد هذا لم يعد بإمكان الأميرة أن تفكر في أي شيء سوى بيضة الرخ .

when Aladdin returned from hunting he found her in a very ill humour

عندما عاد علاء الدين من الصيد وجدها في مزاج سيئ للغاية

He begged to know what was amiss

لقد توسل لمعرفة ما هو الخطأ

and she told him what had spoiled her pleasure

وأخبرته بما أفسد عليها متعتها

"I'm made miserable for the want of a Roc's egg"

"أشعر بالتعاسة بسبب افتقاري إلى بيضة روك "

"If that is all you want you shall soon be happy," replied Aladdin

"إذا كان هذا كل ما تريده فسوف تكون سعيدًا قريبًا"، أجاب علاء الدين

he left her and rubbed the lamp

تركها وفرك المصباح

when the genie appeared he commanded him to bring a Roc's egg

عندما ظهر الجني أمره بإحضار بيضة روك

The genie gave such a loud and terrible shriek that the hall shook

أطلق الجني صرخة عالية ورهيبة لدرجة أن القاعة اهتزت

"Wretch!" he cried, "is it not enough that I have done everything for you?"

"يا أيها البائس !أليس كافيا أنني فعلت كل شيء من أجلك؟ "

"but now you command me to bring my master"

"ولكن الآن تأمرني بإحضار سيدي "

"and you want me to hang him up in the midst of this dome"

"وأنت تريد مني أن أعلقه في وسط هذه القبة "

"You and your wife and your palace deserve to be burnt to ashes"

"أنت وزوجتك وقصرك تستحقون أن تُحرقوا إلى رماد "

"but this request does not come from you"

"ولكن هذا الطلب لا يأتي منك "

"the demand comes from the brother of the magician"

"الطلب يأتي من أخو الساحر "

"the magician whom you have destroyed"

"The magician you destroyed"
"الساحر الذي أهلكته"

"He is now in your palace disguised as the holy woman"
"إنه الآن في قصرك متنكرًا في هيئة المرأة المقدسة"

"the real holy woman he has already murdered"
"المرأة المقدسة الحقيقية التي قتلها بالفعل"

"it was him who put that wish into your wife's head"
"لقد كان هو من وضع هذه الرغبة في رأس زوجتك"

"Take care of yourself, for he means to kill you"
"اعتنِ بنفسك، فهو يريد قتلك"

upon saying this, the genie disappeared
وعند قول هذا اختفى الجني

Aladdin went back to the Princess
عاد علاء الدين إلى الأميرة

he told her that his head ached
أخبرها أن رأسه يؤلمه

so she requested the holy Fatima to be fetched
فطلبت أن يتم إحضار السيدة فاطمة عليها السلام

she could lay her hands on his head
يمكنها أن تضع يديها على رأسه

and his headache would be cured by her powers
وسوف يتم علاج صداعه بقواها

when the magician came near Aladdin seized his dagger
عندما اقترب الساحر استولى علاء الدين على خنجره

and he pierced him in the heart
وطعنه في قلبه

"What have you done?" cried the Princess
"ماذا فعلت؟" صرخت الأميرة

"You have killed the holy woman!"
"لقد قتلت المرأة المقدسة"!

"It is not so," replied Aladdin
"ليس الأمر كذلك" أجاب علاء الدين

"I have killed a wicked magician"
"لقد قتلت ساحرًا شريرًا"

and he told her of how she had been deceived
وأخبرها كيف تم خداعها

After this Aladdin and his wife lived in peace

وبعد ذلك عاش علاء الدين وزوجته في سلام .
He succeeded the Sultan when he died
وخلف السلطان حين توفي
he reigned over the kingdom for many years
لقد حكم المملكة لسنوات عديدة
and he left behind him a long lineage of kings
وترك خلفه سلسلة طويلة من الملوك

The End
النهاية

www.tranzlaty.com

www.ingramcontent.com/pod-product-compliance
Lightning Source LLC
Chambersburg PA
CBHW012010090526
44590CB00026B/3964